CONTENTS

KU-440-769

EDGE BOOKS™

Not Your Ordinary Trivia

MOTORSPORTS TRIVIA

WHAT YOU NEVER KNEW ABOUT CAR RACING, MONSTER TRUCK EVENTS AND MORE MOTOR MANIA

by Joe Tewit

Raintree is an imprint of Capstone Global Library Limited, a company incorporated in England and Wales having its registered office at 264 Banbury Road, Oxford, OX2 7DY – Registered company number: 6695582

www.raintree.co.uk
myorders@raintree.co.uk

Edited by Mandy Robbins
Designed by Juliette Peters
Picture research by Jo Miller
Production by Tori Abraham
Originated by Capstone Global Library Ltd
Printed and bound in India

ISBN 978 1 4747 5946 5
22 21 20 19 18
10 9 8 7 6 5 4 3 2 1

British Library Cataloguing in Publication Data
A full catalogue record for this book is available from the British Library.

Acknowledgements
We would like to thank the following for permission to reproduce photographs: Alamy: Crash Media Group, 7b, Ian Dagnall, 18b, PCN Photography, 19b; AP Images: Andy Newman, 28; Dreamstime: Gorgios, 18t; Getty Images: Heritage Images/Contributor, 8, RacingOne/Contributor, 13; Newscom: WENN/PJA/Paul Jacobs, 27, ZUMA Press/Bill Roth/Adn, 26b, ZUMA Press/Jasen Vinlove, 17t, 19t, ZUMA Press/Jonathan Beck, 23b, ZUMA Press/Marcelo Chello, 17b, ZUMA Press/Vincent Michel, 15t, Icon SMI CBB/Dannie Walls, 14b, USA Today Sports/Mark J. Rebilast, 12; Shutterstock: Action Sports Photography, 14t, AHMAD FAIZAL YAHYA, 6, AlenKadr, 12br, Barry Salmons, 16, Barsan ATTILA, 22, Brian McEntire, 9b, byvalet, 25r, CHEN WS, 25l, Coprid, 12bl, Edu Silva 2ev, 23t, Ev. Safronov, 9t, Faiz Zaki, 10t, Hafiz Johari, 10b, Illerlok_Xolms, 15b, Ioan Panaite, 26t, Ivan Garcia, 7t, JazzyGeoff, 21, Jeff Schultes, 24, LandFox, 29, Mechanik, cover, Serjio74, 11, sippakorn, 20, tcharts, 4
Design elements: Shutterstock: LongQuattro, ShustrikS

The world of motorsports is as varied as the different types of vehicles in it. And everyone involved is itching to find out who will finish first. But you may be surprised to find out some little-known facts about racing.

Modern motorsports began when a French newspaper organized a car race from Paris to Rouen and back in 1894. Since then, motorized racing of many types has zoomed onto the scene.

Many traditions and superstitions have grown up around different motorsports. US driver Dan Gurney was the first person to celebrate a victory by soaking everybody in champagne. He did it in 1967 after winning the 24 Hours of Le Mans race. This celebration quickly became a tradition. Find out more fascinating facts as you speed through these pages.

CHAPTER 1

CAR RACING

The world is full of different types of cars to race. Racers know that timing and technology means the difference between a breathtaking victory or a disheartening defeat.

Formula 1 (F1) cars are some of the fastest in the world. An aeroplane's wings provide lift to keep it flying. But F1 cars use their wings to create **downforce**. This design pushes the cars onto the track. It allows them to take tight corners at high speed. These cars can reach speeds of more than 240 kilometres (150 miles) per hour. The wings create enough force that these cars could be driven upside down along the ceiling of a tunnel!

downforce force of passing air pressing down on a moving vehicle

F1 cars also have better brakes than most other types of cars. This is because they have to slow down and stop from speeds of up to 320 km (200 miles) per hour.

g-force force of gravity on a moving object

F1 drivers have to deal with high **g-forces** while driving. G-forces measure the force of gravity on a moving object. F1 drivers often deal with forces of up to 5G when racing. That means they can feel pressure that is five times more than their body weight. Water is forced from their tear ducts during extreme braking. It sprays across the visors on the inside of their helmets.

David Purley

throttle lever, pedal or handle used to control the speed of an engine

At the 1977 British Grand Prix, driver David Purley faced g-forces higher than any human has ever survived. During a practice lap his **throttle** got stuck open. He crashed soon after, going from 174 km (108 miles) per hour to zero in just two seconds.

Racing driver Niki Lauda won five of the first nine races of the 1976 Formula 1 season. But during the German Grand Prix he had a horrific crash. He was very badly burned, and he was not expected to live. Incredibly, Lauda was back on the racetrack in six weeks. Lauda was leading the drivers' championship by three points before the season's final race in Japan. But he withdrew from that last race. He felt the weather conditions made the race too dangerous. That decision meant that he finished the season in second place. But better to end up in second – and still be alive!

F1 helmets are built to last even in a serious crash. During testing, researchers shoot objects at the helmet's visor. The objects reach speeds of 483 kilometres (300 miles) per hour. If anything leaves a dent deeper than 2.5 millimetres (0.1 inches), the helmet cannot be used.

F1 helmets must protect a driver in case of fire. Testers must prove the gear is up to the challenge. They expose helmets to a flame that is 800 degrees Celsius (1,472 degrees Fahrenheit) for 45 seconds. If the inside of the helmet gets hotter than 70°C (158°F), the helmet cannot be used in a race.

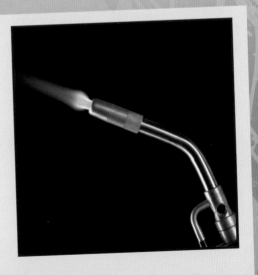

The steering wheels of F1 cars have a secret weapon. When a driver is close to the car ahead, he or she can press a button for a boost. This changes the angle of a rear wing flap. The change lessens wind **resistance** and increases speed temporarily. It's what allows a driver to pass the car in front.

The tyres of F1 racing cars create a lot of **friction** with the racetrack. These tyres become scalding hot during a race. Even after the race, a car's tyres can be as hot as 120°C (248°F). That's hot enough to fry an egg!

The Monaco Grand Prix is one of the premier races in F1. Drivers race through the city streets. Workers weld down manhole covers along the track before this race. Otherwise, the suction created by the downforce of the F1 cars would rip them right out of the ground.

resistance force that opposes or slows the motion of an object

friction force produced when two objects rub against each other; friction slows down objects

Indy car racing is a motorsport in the United States. Indy cars are capable of extreme straight-line speed. They also have a push-to-pass button on the steering wheel. This gives drivers extra speed for a few moments. Drivers may use this extra speed to pass someone. Or they may try to make sure another driver can't pass them.

Drinking milk after an Indy 500 win is an honoured tradition. It started in 1936. Louis Meyer won the race that year. His mother had told him buttermilk would cool him down after a hot day on the racetrack. Emerson Fittipaldi broke the tradition when he won in 1993. He drank orange juice instead. This drink was a nod to his family's orange tree business.

John, Michael, Jeff and Mario Andretti

The Andretti family is legendary when it comes to racing. But they almost always have bad luck at the Indy 500. Mario Andretti won the race in 1969. But no one in his family has won it since. Something always seems to go wrong. The 1992 Indy 500 was particularly bad. All four Andrettis in the race faced bad luck. Mario and his son Jeff both left the race with broken bones. Mario's nephew John crashed into a pile of tyres during a pit stop. And Mario's son Michael met misfortune too. He was leading the field at lap 189 of the 200-lap race. But then he had to retire from the race because of a failed fuel pump.

In 2001, Tony Stewart became the only driver to complete a combined 1,770 km (1,100 miles) of two major races in just one day. He drove to sixth place at the Indy 500. Then he travelled by plane to Charlotte, North Carolina. That's where he finished in third place at the Coca-Cola 600.

Top-fuel dragsters speed up faster than any other type of car in the world. These 10-metre (33-foot) long cars guzzle 57 litres (15 gallons) of fuel in a single 3.7-second run. An average car could cover 917 km (570 miles) using the same amount of fuel.

The 2010 winners of the 24 Hours of Le Mans

Anchorage, Alaska

Brooklyn, New York

The 24 Hours of Le Mans race is the oldest endurance car race in the world. Three-person teams take turns racing a car for one full day. They drive as far as they can in that time. In 2010 a team set the record for the most distance covered in the 24-hour period. They drove 5,410 km (3,360 miles). That's more than six times the length of the Indy 500. It's almost the distance from Brooklyn, New York, to Anchorage, Alaska!

CHAPTER 2

MONSTER TRUCK EVENTS

Monster truck races are one type of monster truck event. In these races pairs of trucks compete side-by-side on the same track. They drive around and over obstacles in a timed race. It takes eight people working 20 hours over three days to make the tracks and jumps necessary for a Monster Jam event.

Monster trucks are about 3.7 metres (12 feet) tall and 3.7 metres (12 feet) wide. A monster truck weighs as much as a large Asian elephant. Their high-powered engines help drivers to make them do tricks such as wheelies and backflips.

Monster trucks weigh up to 5,443 kilograms (12,000 pounds). But they can launch off of high ramps. They jump up to 9 metres (30 feet) in the air. BIGFOOT #18 holds the record for the longest jump at more than 65 metres (214 feet)!

Monster Jam trucks don't have doors. Any doors you can see on the sides are only painted on. To get inside, drivers have to climb in through a space underneath the truck.

Monster trucks crush roughly 3,000 cars each year. But they don't stop at cars. Vans, buses, ambulances and even aeroplanes get stomped on too.

In the late 1980s, many people were trying to build the biggest machine possible. Bob Chandler topped them all. He found a set of Firestone Tundra tyres in a Seattle scrapyard. He bolted the 3-metre (10-foot) tyres onto BIGFOOT #5. This giant vehicle still holds the Guinness World Record for the world's tallest and widest pickup truck.

Bob Chandler also owned the original BIGFOOT truck. But it doesn't look anything like the mythical Bigfoot creature. This giant truck got its name from how hard Chandler would stomp on the accelerator pedal.

Monster trucks create an amazing 1,500 **horsepower.** A special blower forces air and fuel into their engines. An average four-door car has less than 300 horsepower.

horsepower unit for measuring an engine's power

CHAPTER 3

MOTORCYCLE RACING

Motorcycle racing is risky. There is no frame around the vehicle to protect riders. Motorcycles have powerful engines. Riders zip down paved or dirt tracks. Some even do backflips and other tricks.

The Isle of Man TT is the most dangerous motorcycle race in the world. The racecourse goes over steep hills and through thick forests. It also includes public roads in many places. For years, that was a problem. Racer Archie Birkin died in 1927 after swerving to avoid a fish cart. Now the roads are closed to the public during the practice and the race. But the course is still risky. More than 145 racers have died in the event since 1907.

American motocross rider Alex Harvill achieved the world's longest ramp-to-dirt motorcycle jump on 12 May 2012. The gap between his take-off and landing ramp was 108 metres (354 feet). The jump itself was an incredible 130 metres (425 feet).

Enduro is a type of motorcycle race run over long cross-country courses. These off-road races can last for several days. Riders must be ready to drive through several types of terrain, including sand and mud. Unlike other races, enduro is not about finishing first. It's about meeting **checkpoints** and finishing a race at a preset time.

checkpoint place where race vehicles are stopped for official identification

Freestyle motocross riders travel up tall ramps and perform wild stunts. Safety gear is a must in such a risky sport. And that gear gets heavy. Riders wear helmets, chest and back protection, boots, a neck brace and gloves. That gear adds up to about 10 kilograms (23 pounds). That's like carrying a 1-year-old baby around on a motorcycle!

MotoTrials are the ultimate in balance on a motorcycle. Competitors try to complete a course that crosses streams, fallen trees, huge rocks and steep slopes. The rider whose feet touch the ground the least is the winner.

CHAPTER 4

RATHER RANDOM RACES

From aeroplanes to **hovercraft**, if a vehicle can be raced, there are people doing it. Discover fascinating facts about some unusual types of motor racing.

The National Championship Air Races in Nevada, USA, are the world's fastest races. Planes in the unlimited class round courses at speeds of more than 724 km (450 miles) per hour. Reno Air Race courses go around the outside of a series of telephone poles 15 m (50 feet) tall. Course officials make sure passing planes don't cheat and cut inside the course poles.

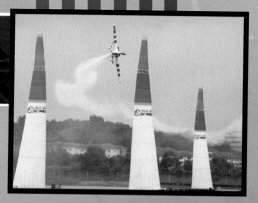

Pilots at the Red Bull Air Race score points by flying through sets of **pylons** 25 m (82 feet) tall. They have to turn sideways to squeeze through some of the pylons. When they do that their planes are in a **freefall**. Red Bull Air Race pylons are inflated with air. They deflate instantly if a passing plane touches them.

Drone racers don't have a vehicle to ride on or in. They use goggles with first-person views to see the racecourse. The brightly lit drones can reach speeds of up to 129 km (80 miles) per hour. Many indoor races happen in warehouses. In these races speeds stay below 97 km (60 miles) per hour.

hovercraft vehicle that travels on a cushion of air over both land and water

pylon marking post for guiding aircraft pilots

freefall descend through the atmosphere for a time without the aid of a parachute

drone unmanned, remote-controlled aircraft

The Iron Dog is a race that's about more than speed. It's also about survival. Racers drive snowmobiles through the Alaskan wilderness. The frozen course is more than 3,200 km (2,000 miles) long. The winner usually takes 8 to 10 days to finish the race. The race is so dangerous that racers have to travel in pairs. Each person has a snowmobile. Checkpoints are spaced up to 190 km (120 miles) apart. Each racer also carries 2.3 kg (5 pounds) of tools in case of breakdowns. If they want to get some sleep, racers curl up in sleeping bags designed to handle sub-zero temperatures.

Iron Dog racers can face temperatures of -49°C (-57°F). Wet feet can lead to frostbite. Racers wear uncomfortable boots to keep their feet dry while riding in extreme weather. Even if water gets poured down the inside of the boot, the design keeps the foot dry.

The British Lawn Mower Racing Association hosts an annual race. Drivers race on lawn mowers for 12 hours. Most of the race happens in darkness. Skilled drivers can hit speeds of 80 km (50 miles) per hour on straight parts of the track. To keep racers safe, there aren't any blades in the mowers.

In the 1960s, large boats raced on long courses over the open ocean. Open-ocean boats are more than 13 metres (45 feet) long. They have three or four engines. One of the most popular races was an 800-km (500-mile) race around the Bahamas. Today, courses are only 9.6 to 16 km (6 to 10 miles) long. Boats race just off shore so that more people can see the competing boats.

Hydroplane drag boats speed over the water on a cushion of air. Only their propeller and two back edges actually touch the surface. Boats in the Unlimited Class are the fastest. According to the American Power Boat Association, Dave Vilwock set the world speed record in the Unlimited Class at 354.9 km (220.5 miles) per hour in 2004.

Hovercrafts ride on a cushion of air, giving rise to a new form of vehicle – the air-cushion vehicle (ACV). In the UK, the Hovercraft Club of Great Britain organizes the world's only hovercraft racing championship. These machines navigate racecourses that cover both land and water.

Glossary

checkpoint place where race vehicles are stopped for official identification

downforce force of passing air pressing down on a moving vehicle

drone unmanned, remote-controlled aircraft

freefall descend through the atmosphere for a time without the aid of a parachute

friction force produced when two objects rub against each other; friction slows down objects

g-force force of gravity on a moving object

horsepower unit for measuring an engine's power

hovercraft vehicle that travels on a cushion of air over both land and water

pylon marking post for guiding aircraft pilots

resistance force that opposes or slows the motion of an object

throttle lever, pedal or handle used to control the speed of an engine

Find out more

Books

Car Science: A White-Knuckle Guide to Science in Action,
Richard Hammond (DK Children, 2011)

Motor Sports (Fantastic Sport Facts), Michael Hurley
(Raintree, 2014)

The World's Fastest Motorcycles (World Record Breakers),
Ashley Norris (Raintree, 2017)

Websites

www.brooklandsmuseum.com/explore/our-history/motor-racing
Learn about the world's first purpose-built motor racing circuit.

www.dkfindout.com/uk/transport/history-cars/racing-cars
Find out more about the history of racing cars.

Index